Original title:
Beneath the Water's Surface

Copyright © 2025 Creative Arts Management OÜ
All rights reserved.

Author: Charles Whitfield
ISBN HARDBACK: 978-1-80587-370-9
ISBN PAPERBACK: 978-1-80587-840-7

The Shadows' Serenade

In the deep where fish wear hats,
A crab recites its silly chats.
Jellyfish dance with glowing pride,
While sea turtles roll, their flippers wide.

Octopuses juggle seaweed snacks,
And seahorses ride on stingray backs.
The clownfish swim in comical lines,
Ticking off time with ticklish signs.

Depths Whispering Secrets

The angler fish with a crooked light,
Flashes smiles, but gives quite a fright.
Anemones wave like they got moves,
While oyster laughs at all the grooves.

Dancing zooplankton swim in glee,
Joking about a new VIP.
Salty sea jokes flow all around,
As fish form bands with a crazy sound.

Unseen Realms of the Sea

A hermit crab in a shiny shell,
Claims it's a castle, oh what a sell!
Pufferfish puff up all day long,
Making bubbles to go with the song.

A shrimp with bling struts down the lane,
Singing tales of the ocean's fame.
The seaweed waves, a dancing crew,
As they laugh at the clumsy blue.

The Call of the Abyss

Deep down where the oddballs reside,
A dolphin cracks jokes, full of pride.
A whale on a chair, sipping on tea,
Says, 'This sea life is simply for me!'

Starfish roll over, tickled by sand,
While crabs play cards, a silly band.
The sounds of laughter rise and swell,
In this hidden world where the sea critters dwell.

Currents of the Forgotten

Fish in tuxedos dance with glee,
A clam's ball; oh, what a spree!
Octopus plays the ukulele,
Sardines sing, their tunes so fray.

Anemones wear wigs so bright,
Tickling crabs in a comical fight.
Seahorses gossip, what a sight!
Their tiny tales take flight each night.

The Silence of Submerged Dreams

Starfish dreaming of pizza pies,
Bubble-blowing with big round eyes.
A whale jokes, 'I am no small fry,'
While mermaids giggle, 'Oh, my, oh my!'

Squids in shades float by with flair,
Jellyfish twirl without a care.
Turtles debating the best hair,
All under the still, shimmering air.

Mysterious Depths Await

Eels in whispers share their schemes,
Making waves with their wild dreams.
A dolphin, stealthy, silently beams,
Joking, 'Have you seen my ice creams?'

Coral reefs gossip with loud cracks,
Pufferfish puff, avoid all attacks.
Crabs in tuxes, on curious tracks,
With sea cucumbers forming acts.

Cryptic Murmurs Underneath

A treasure chest filled with socks,
Mermaids chuckle, 'Let's see who rocks!'
Barracudas play hopscotch in flocks,
While snails host a race around the docks.

A chorus of bubbles sings out loud,
Fish forming a wobbly crowd.
They cheer for the jester—oh so proud,
As octopuses dance, drawing a crowd.

Glimmers of Life Below

Fish wearing hats, oh what a sight,
Dancing like bubbles, full of delight.
A crab plays chess with a wise old eel,
While jellyfish giggle, it's quite the deal.

Seahorses twirl in a waltz so grand,
Cormorants cluck at the fun on land.
Starfish make wishes on shells with a grin,
And the clams chant songs with their pearls tucked in.

Depths of Serenity

Octopuses juggle, they have such flair,
With eight hands moving, it's quite the affair.
Pufferfish puff up, they think they're so cool,
While turtles slow dance, breaking all type of rule.

Scooters made of fins in a race so bold,
Crabs sprint in jeans that make 'em look old.
Anemones giggle as they sway to the beat,
While clownfish tease, saying, "Hey, look, we're neat!"

The Alchemy of Underwater Worlds

Mermaids bake cookies with seaweed for dough,
While dolphins share secrets we'd never know.
A fish paints portraits in colors so bright,
And all the sea turtles grin in delight.

Coral reefs sparkle like jewelry at night,
As sea cucumbers dance in sheer delight.
They mix up a potion from bubbles and sand,
And send all the crabs to a floating band.

Swimming in Forgotten Whispers

Lost treasure chests filled with socks and old shoes,
Pirates swim past, always spreading the news.
Scallops wear sunglasses, they're cooler than cool,
With a wink and a wave, they break all the rules.

Old shipwrecks tell stories of days filled with cheer,
While barnacles gossip, "I hear they're quite near!"
A whale sings a tune that makes seahorses dance,
As fish join the chorus in a silly romance.

The Hidden World

In a fishy cafe, they gather to chat,
Seahorses sipping lattes, imagine that!
Jellyfish in pajamas, looking quite spry,
Squid crack jokes as the octopus sighs.

Mermaids are ordering pizza today,
With toppings of seaweed, it's quite the buffet!
A crab in a bowtie knows all the best spots,
While oysters are gossiping over lost thoughts.

Below the Brimming Surface

A clam tried to dance, but it wobbled too much,
Twirl and then stumble, oh what a touch!
Pufferfish laughing, they're such a delight,
While turtles are practicing moves by moonlight.

In the current, a fish with a top hat so grand,
Debates with a whale about who rules the band.
The shrimp with a trumpet adds flair to the show,
While sea cucumbers lend a soft glow.

Notes of the Undercurrent

Tadpoles in tuxedos, they dance with great flair,
Toilet paper fish, watch out for their snare!
Grouchy old eels, with their grumpy old frowns,
While plankton wear crowns, king of their towns.

Anemones twirl; it's a colorful dream,
While clownfish make jokes, all part of the theme.
With a wink and a wave, they swim right along,
Creating a symphony, nature's own song.

Embrace of the Deep

Nautilus wearing glasses, a scholar, it seems,
Calculates currents and sometimes daydreams.
A dolphin plays chess with a curious seal,
While starfish debate if they should dance or squeal.

In a bubble of giggles, the wrasses convene,
Plotting a prank that's fit for a queen.
Tangled in seaweed, they giggle and twirl,
What a whimsical world, this oceanic whirl!

Lurking in the Blue

Fish in tuxedos, oh what a sight,
They spin and twirl, in the soft moonlight.
A crab wearing glasses, quite the scholar,
As a foolfish flops, causing great laughter.

Octopus juggling, with arms on parade,
While seaweed dances, in a watery fade.
A shrimp with a trumpet, plays tunes quite absurd,
As the sea whispers secrets, like an old bird.

Murmurs from the Depths

Whispers of bubbles, secrets they share,
A dolphin playing tag, with flair and a dare.
Clams gossip loudly, pearls stuck in their jaw,
While a grouchy old eel grumbles, 'Ain't this raw?'

A starfish flipping, trying to be cool,
As jellyfish dance like they're in a school.
A porcupine puffer, proud of his spikes,
Laughs at the angler, with all of his likes.

Tides of Mystery

Seahorses tango, in a wild waltz flow,
While a turtle complains, 'This dance is so slow!'
A clam with a monocle, looks smart but is shy,
As a rogue little minnow just swims on by.

A whale with a top hat, sings songs of the sea,
While the fish give a cheer, 'What a roar, oh me!'
A sea urchin chuckles, with spines all aglow,
As tides tick and tock, in this topsy-turvy show.

Silent Realms Below

A bubble parade, floats past on a whim,
As barnacles chat, all grumpy and grim.
Anemones giggle, dressed up for a date,
While a confused crab, tries just to relate.

Flounders play hide and seek, in the sand,
As a whale gives a wink, isn't life grand?
With sea cucumbers chuckling, their tales so goofy,
These silent realms burst with laughter so loony.

Echoes of Liquid Dreams

Fish in tuxedos dance and twirl,
Waltzing around with a seaweed girl.
An octopus plays the grand piano,
Singing of water and a lost flamingo.

Crabs wearing glasses read the news,
While jellybeans take a casual snooze.
A dolphin juggles with seashells bright,
Making waves of laughter in the moonlight.

Seahorses gossip, tails intertwined,
Claiming the ocean's the best place to unwind.
Turtles in shade toss popcorn grains,
Sharing jokes that wash away the pains.

When the anchor drops, the fish all cheer,
"Let's throw a party, the humans are near!"
Mermaids bubble with giggles and tunes,
While singing starfish sway under the moons.

Secrets of the Abyss

In the depths where the fish are aloof,
Squid secretly record every goof.
A pufferfish starts a comedy show,
Inflating with laughter, stealing the glow.

Crab clowns juggling with shells and glee,
Whispers of pranks drift through the sea.
The angler's light reveals a silly sight,
A crab in a wig, oh what a fright!

Ghostly eels in a conga line,
With each slick move, they perfectly shine.
Turtles on surfboards catching some rays,
Surfing the currents in a silly craze.

As tides rise and whirl, the laughter grows,
Secrets of the abyss, only ocean knows.
With bubbles and giggles, they share their tales,
Under the waves where joy never fails.

The Veil of Aquatic Shadows

In shadows where fish play peek-a-boo,
A flounder delivers the evening news.
With a flip and a splash, they make a scene,
Shadows dance wildly, creating a sheen.

A whale in disguise dons a party hat,
Sings a solo, "How 'bout that?"
Starfish tap-dancing on a giant shell,
With all of their friends, they ring the bell.

Sharks wear disguises that boggle the mind,
As they sneak into parties, truly unkind.
Anemones giggle with such liveliness,
Proclaiming their jig is the ultimate bliss.

As the tide pulls back, the ocean breathes,
Whirling in laughter, it never leaves.
With shadows and starlight, the fun won't cease,
In a world of enchantment, there's always peace.

Currents of Hidden Depths

Turtles in tutus and dolphins that dance,
Flipping through currents, taking a chance.
Bubble-blowing contests and stingray races,
Underwater parties in whimsical places.

Clams with bling bling in pearly shells,
Cheering each other with rhythmic bells.
Horseshoe crabs beat the drum with zeal,
Creating a symphony that makes them squeal.

The sea cucumber hosts a karaoke night,
Where fish belt out tunes, feeling just right.
With gill-swaying motions, they sing out loud,
As nature's orchestra plays for the crowd.

In currents of laughter, they splash and swoop,
Making the ocean a jubilant loop.
With whimsies of water, they frolic and play,
In hidden depths, joy finds its way.

A Canvas of Aquatic Shadows

In the pond, a frog took a dive,
Painting sketches of fish that arrive.
With a splash and a glee, he went on a spree,
Chasing bubbles, feeling alive.

The goldfish giggled in their jeweled attire,
As the clownfish danced, sparking desire.
They twirled 'round a rock,
In a wacky sea sock,
While the seaweed swayed to their choir.

A crab tried to salsa, with two left feet,
Clumsy movements, oh so offbeat!
He tripped with a clank,
Then sank with a prank,
Turning the tide into quite the feat.

As shrimp called to lobsters, who's winning the race?
They floated and flopped, a comical chase.
With each silly flip,
They embraced their own trip,
In this watery world, fun was the base.

Ripples of the Unseen

A turtle named Tim wore glasses too small,
Trying to read at the coral-lined hall.
With a wink and a grin,
He'd squint, then dive in,
Chasing down shrimp to find wisdom after all!

The octopus chef, with eight arms in play,
Cooked up a storm in an extravagant way.
His recipe plans,
With crabs on the pans,
Made the seahorses squeal, 'What a buffet!'

A whale often joked, with a laugh like a boom,
While tickling fish as they glided past gloom.
'It's a party, my friend,
Let the good times extend!'
And the school danced and swayed, in aquatic room.

Down in the depths, where the goblins napped,
A mermaid laughed loud; her humor was wrapped.
She played tricks so sly,
Like a wise guy,
Making bubbles burst, as everyone clapped.

Whispers in the Deep

A jellyfish floated, feeling quite slick,
Spreading tales of the ocean, oh so thick.
He spoke of a shark,
Who fancied a lark,
In a tutu, to mimic the ball and the tick.

Clams held their breath, in a fitted shell suit,
Their gossip and chatter undoubtedly cute.
'Have you seen that brave fish?
He makes quite a wish,
To dance with a wave instead of a flute!'

The anglerfish grinned, with a light in his gaze,
While cracking up jokes in a luminous haze.
With a flick of his fin,
He'd reel them all in,
With humor that sparkled in fanciful ways.

A dolphin named Dot, swung by for a laugh,
Playing tag with the rays in a bubble bath.
With flips and with spins,
They shared silly wins,
Stirring up joy as they splashed in half.

Secrets in Aquatic Halls

Fish gather gossip, as they turn and swirl,
Octopus ink spills secrets, quite the underwater whirl.
Coral reefs giggle, some jokes flow with grace,
While jellyfish dance in an electric embrace.

Clams flash their pearls, boasting in the sand,
Starfish hold meetings, discussing the land.
A crustacean's banter makes shells crack a smile,
Bubbles of laughter drift up for a mile!

Whale songs echo, full of playful delight,
Echoes of mariners still lost in the night.
Seahorses gossip, entwined in a spin,
Flipping their tails, where the fun will begin.

Mermaids do cartwheels, bobbing with flair,
Tickling the fins of fish, floating in air.
With a splash and a giggle, the ocean comes alive,
In this watery realm, where the chuckles thrive!

The Language of Tides

Waves whisper secrets, pulling on the shore,
As crabs tap dance, always wanting more.
The gulls tell tales, flapping wings in jest,
While dolphins perform, trying to impress!

Sandcastles sigh as incoming waves tease,
Shells hold the stories of sun and breeze.
A starfish thinks deep, pondering a joke,
While snails plan a race, but nobody's woke!

Rock pools are theatres, where shrimp play their part,
With laughs and their antics, they're masters of art.
The tide plays the music, a shimmering beat,
From the surface above, to where creatures meet.

So tune into giggles that flow from the sea,
A language of laughter that's wild and free.
In this watery world where antics abound,
The fun never stops, it's a joy we have found!

Enigmas of the Abyss

In the deep dark corners, where light takes a peek,
Creatures conspire, sharing tales unique.
The anglerfish grins, with his lantern aglow,
A mystery unfolds, in the depths below.

Squid hold conventions, with arms all a-flail,
Debating the best in a wiggly tale.
While worms dig their tunnels, creating a fuss,
"Who's got the finest, the smartest of us?"

In silence they shiver, it's a game of charades,
Testing their talents in shifting cascades.
A sea cucumber jokes, being a lazy old chap,
While the pufferfish bursts, "This dance is a snap!"

With a wink and a wave, they hide 'neath the foam,
In their enigmatic realm, they've made it their home.
So next time you ponder what's down in the deep,
Remember the giggles that secrets can keep!

Treasures in the Brine

Nuggets of laughter lie hidden in shells,
With barnacle buddies, sharing their spells.
The crabs spin their yarns, pinching just right,
A feast for the giggles, in the cool moonlight.

Oysters are striking, their pearls gleam with glee,
They chuckle and chortle, "Come dive in with me!"
Seaweed's a jester, draped over the rocks,
Tickling the fish as they swim in flocks.

Piggies dive down for a treasure so fine,
Finding lost spoons and an old pirate's wine.
The dolphins throw parties, with bubbles galore,
Inviting the mermaids to dance on the shore.

From krill to the whales, there's mischief in play,
As treasures of laughter continue to sway.
In this briny deep, the joy won't rescind,
As the sea holds its secrets, and tickles the Finn!

The Lure of Hidden Depths

Down below the waves, a fish wears a hat,
Doing the cha-cha with a curious cat.
A crab tells a joke, its claws in the air,
While dolphins dance round in a cheeky affair.

An octopus tries to juggle some shells,
But drops them like anchors, oh, what a spell!
A turtle rolls by, with a grin so wide,
It sings to the seahorse, a karaoke tide.

The seaweed sways, joins the slapdash dance,
While starfish boogie without a second chance.
And somewhere, a clam gives a wink with a grin,
As sea life rejoices in this ocean spin.

So if you dive down, bring your laughter and cheer,
Join the underwater party, the fun's always near!

Beneath the Moondrenched Waves

A walrus in shades thinks he's quite the cool,
   Sipping on seaweed in a puffed-up pool.
A mermaid named Myrtle, she twirls with glee,
   While fish all around roll eyes, oh whee!

The moonlight shimmer brings starfish to prance,
   With clams in tuxedos, they start a quick dance.
With a flip and a splash, they laugh in the tide,
   Creating a splashy, wet, silly ride.

A dolphin debates with a wise old crab,
   Who's better at jokes, or just needs a fab?
The laughs echo loud in the silvery light,
   Making the ocean seem dizzy with delight!

As waves crash and break, they join in the fun,
   With bubbles that tickle, oh what a run!

Tales from the Twilight Tides

In the twilight glow, a fish sings a song,
While a clam starts to tap to the beat all along.
The squid pulls a prank, squirts ink with a grin,
As eels pull a heist to steal dinner again.

A seagull pelican, with feathers so grand,
Wants to join in the fun — the sea's his band.
He flaps and he flops, trying hard to dive,
But ends up in seaweed — just feeling alive.

A crab wears a necklace made of bright shells,
While jellyfish twirl in a delicate swell.
With tales of adventure that twist in the light,
These underwater critters are quite the delight.

And thus the tide whispers of laughter and cheer,
Where fish tell tall tales, and the sea is their seer.

Secret Gardens of the Ocean Floor

In gardens of seaweed, a fish sprays cologne,
Declaring it's fresher than any sea throne.
A pufferfish struts with a nonchalant flair,
While snails slip and slide without any care.

A slug in a tux gives a wink and a nod,
To the starfish brigade who dance like a god.
They twirl on the reef with a sparkle and twist,
The ocean's a stage, and they can't be missed!

With laughter that bubbles from corals so bright,
Anemones tickle in pure moonlit night.
And clam shells are clapping, it's quite the charade,
In this jolly demesne where wonders parade.

So join in the fun at the ocean's own door,
There's magic in laughter, who could ask for more?

Pictures of Undersea Wonders

A fish in a tux, what a sight,
He dances and twirls, oh so right.
With a shrimp as his date, they do twine,
Under the disco ball, they shine.

A crab sporting shades, he can't see,
Trying to groove, but he's stuck on a bee.
The seaweed sways with laughter so loud,
As jellyfish float, all wrapped in a cloud.

A dolphin in sneakers tries to race,
Stumbles and tumbles, oh what a chase.
But who could resist such a comical show?
The octopus waves like a pro in a row.

With pinches of salt and a splash of mirth,
These finned friends know how to have worth.
In this watery realm, joy takes its chance,
For humor and bubbles create the best dance.

Voices of the Ocean's Embrace

Whales sing a tune, quite out of key,
Their chorus a blend, delightful yet free.
A clam starts to hum, but forgets the note,
While turtles just laugh, on their shells they float.

Starfish tell tales of their past misdeeds,
Like missing their points in sandy weeds.
With wit and a wink, they share their lore,
As fish roll their eyes, always wanting more.

The octopus jokes with eight arms to spare,
Making shadow puppets, in water's cool air.
While sea cucumbers sit, feeling wise,
Dropping old wisdom and cringing at lies.

A sea urchin grumbles, "Life's just a prick,"
As the sea horse prances, doing a kick.
Beneath this blue dome, where laughter's the aim,
The ocean's embrace is a whimsical game.

Fables from the Depths

Once a fish dreamed to learn how to fly,
He flapped his tail, and aimed for the sky.
With bubbles of hope and a splash of zest,
He landed on clouds, escaping the jest.

A turtle named Larry in a top hat doth stroll,
Claiming he's fast, on a slow-motion roll.
The gulls scoff and caw, "What a peculiar sight!"
As he puffs on a bubble, feeling so bright.

An eel twists and shouts, "I'm really quite sleek,
I can dance like a pro, give the choreo a peek!"
But he trips on a rock, and oh what a clatter,
All the clownfish giggle, "It's just a matter!"

A shark with a grin, wearing glasses so round,
Says, "I'm on a diet, but truthfully, I've found,
A plankton buffet—endless delight!
Let's dive for a feast, now it feels right!"

Currents of Forgotten Dreams

A seahorse dreams of being a knight,
Charging through currents, ready to fight.
With a shell for a shield and a spear made of sea,
All he needs now is a sidekick—like me!

A stagnant old log claims he was once grand,
"Fame!" he exclaims, with a wave of his hand.
But the fish just roll eyes, avoiding his tale,
While shrimp giggle close, shaking their tails.

Anemones sway, with stories untold,
Whispering secrets of treasures of old.
But every time a crab bends to lend an ear,
They forget the narrative, instead, drink a beer.

With waves full of chuckles in deep-blue allure,
These currents of dreams add laughter for sure.
In the humor of depths, we find what's divine,
With fish in the limelight, it's all quite fine.

Portraits of a Watery World

Bubbles pop and fish do stare,
With silly grins and goofy flair.
Octopus paints with splashes bright,
Claiming his fame in the moonlight.

Crabs wearing hats of kelp and shells,
Dance like they've escaped their wells.
Seahorses prance in a conga line,
While starfish munch on snacks divine.

Turtles giggle as they glide,
In snappy suits, they take a ride.
Anemones tickle, making a fuss,
In this watery realm, it's all a plus.

With fishes gossiping, tales to share,
Under the waves, without a care.
Splashing fun in a vibrant scene,
Life's a joke, or so it seems.

The Soft Touch of Drowned Realities

Mermaids sing with voices high,
While dolphins give a cheeky sigh.
Jellyfish float in cotton candy,
Poking fun at fish named Sandy.

Clams hold secrets with a grin,
While seaweed sways, flaunting its spin.
Eels try hard to look so slick,
But end up tangled, oh so quick!

Cranky lobster, dressed in style,
Waves hello with a grumpy smile.
The deep-sea party's quite a sight,
As fishes dance all through the night.

Whale calls echo, a comic tune,
Echoes bouncing, afternoon.
In this kingdom, so absurd,
Life's a laugh, just as I heard.

Traces of Time in the Liquid Echo

Sea urchins play their thorny game,
While old shipwrecks are never the same.
Barnacles mumble their ancient lore,
As mermaids eat popcorn on the floor.

Treasure chests filled with shiny bits,
Pirate ghosts playing hide and splits.
Squids ink jokes from long ago,
Tickling fish with a playful show.

Crabby complaints from a sunken ship,
As dolphins take a wild dip.
The deep sea echoes with laughter loud,
A wacky ocean, proud and endowed!

Rusty anchors, tales of glee,
In their embrace, all fish are free.
Time's a joke in this watery toast,
To the funny things we love the most.

Lost Chronicles of the Deep

Once a pirate with a parrot bright,
Lost his hat in a whirlpool fight.
Now fish sport it with great delight,
"A treasure!" they shout, "What a sight!"

Shells gossip through coral towns,
While blowfish blow up with frowns.
Turtles telling tales of swashbuckles,
As sea cucumbers share their chuckles.

The wrecks of ships host parties grand,
A conga line, it's quite unplanned.
Eels boogie with outlandish grace,
Though they trip, they still keep pace.

In the depths where the sun shines rare,
Life's a circus without a care.
Flip a fin, share a grin,
In this deep dive, let the laughter begin!

The Dance of the Veiled Currents

In the depths where fishies twirl,
A crab's doing its fancy swirl.
Seahorses laugh, in pairs they swing,
While octopuses play a game of fling.

A turtle trips on a seaweed strand,
And jellyfish float, quite unplanned.
Snails in tuxedos glide with grace,
What a sight in this watery place!

A clownfish tells the best of jokes,
While gobies giggle, the silliest folks.
With bubbles popping left and right,
They dance through currents, a merry sight!

As waves tickle, they cheer and cheer,
In this anemone, no room for fear.
With fins and flippers, off they dash,
A water party, a bubbly bash!

Fantasies in the Wet Darkness

In shadows deep, where creatures play,
A fishy bard sings night and day.
Starfish claps, in rhythm they sway,
As squids toss ink in a playful display.

An eel slides by, with a cheesy grin,
Dancing with clams, oh what a din!
Drifting along, with laughter they spin,
In the dark, where the fun won't thin.

Sea turtles telling tales so grand,
While crabs break out in a funny band.
A pufferfish tries to join the flow,
But puffs up big, much to its woe!

With plankton glowing, they twirl and glide,
Through laughter and giggles, they take a ride.
In the wetness where dreams take flight,
They dance through darkness, oh what delight!

Where the Light Fades Away

When sunlight dims and shadows grow,
A dolphin's leap causes quite a show.
Glowing creatures twinkle and glide,
As silly seagulls caw and slide.

A lobster with disco shades appears,
While sea turtles toast with fishy cheers.
"Dance with us!" they shout, full of zest,
As the seaweed wiggles, never let it rest!

The dark is bright—what a crazy scheme!
With whispers of bubbles, they dance and beam.
In this twilight realm, no room for gloom,
Just mermaids ready to twirl and zoom!

As the waves chuckle, they all unite,
A jamboree in the fading light.
In this inky sea, where giggles overflow,
They spin and sway, putting on a show!

Treasures of the Silent Abyss

In the calm where secrets blend,
A treasure chest gives up a friend.
A friendly crab pops out with glee,
As pearls laugh, "Oh, come play with me!"

Invisible rafts of plankton drift,
The chorus of bubbles, a rhythmic gift.
A sea cucumber with a pose so grand,
Once it stood tall, now it's just bland!

Glimmers of humor in the deep,
Octopuses twirl, they don't lose sleep.
With tangled legs in a goofy mess,
They giggle at fish who wear a dress!

In this quiet realm, so full of surprise,
Where silliness reigns and laughter never dies.
Together they frolic, none ever alone,
In watery depths, they've truly grown!

The Dance of Forgotten Echoes

In the depths where fish compete,
A clam can tap its toe to beat.
Jellyfish swing with all their grace,
Wobbling in this underwater space.

Starfish gather for a snack,
Dropping moves that few can track.
Seahorses twirl in fancy styles,
As seaweed sways and plays with smiles.

An octopus shows off a flair,
With eight arms waving in the air.
Crabs clap shells like castanets,
While the sea turtle makes no bets.

With every splash, they cheer and shout,
Who knew the ocean was about?
In this realm of bobbing bliss,
The dance of echoes, a soggy kiss.

Deep Beneath the Thalassic Cradle

A fish with goggles takes a dive,
While anemones dance, feeling alive.
The playful dolphins make a fuss,
Bumping into a curious bus.

A shrimp in shoes, oh what a sight,
Tap-dances under the moon's soft light.
Bubble-blowing pufferfish puff,
While grumpy groupers act quite tough.

Coral reefs become a stage,
Where sea creatures unleash their rage.
Clownfish giggle as they embrace,
The slapstick charm of this wild place.

A sea turtle yawns, "Please don't be late!"
"Don't rush, my finned friends, let's celebrate!"
As barnacles sing in the background,
The melody of humor's profound.

Hidden Lore of the Mysterious Deep

In the swirls of ocean's brew,
Lurks a monster known to few.
But rather than causing fright,
He juggles fish—what a sight!

The wise old crab, all snug and nice,
Tells tales of clams and their paradise.
Whale songs echo, full of cheer,
About a sea star's high career.

An anglerfish dons a hat of gay,
While otters roll and play all day.
Nudibranchs strut their vibrant clothes,
Dancing as if to strike a pose.

These beings hidden from the sun,
Enjoying life and having fun.
For down below, where few have peered,
A world of laughter is revered.

The Timeless Dance Beneath

Electric eels sway with a buzz,
While clownfish laugh and make a fuzz.
The seagrass forms a perfect floor,
Where every creature wants to score.

Crabs do the shuffle, all in line,
Catching rhythm just like fine wine.
With a wiggle and a shake, they boast,
Competing to see who can coast.

A flounder flips with a wink and smile,
Preparing to dance in underwater style.
The groupers cheer, it's quite a show,
As waves of laughter start to flow.

In this realm of splashes and cheers,
All creatures forgot their decades of fears.
For here in the depths, where humor beats,
The dance goes on—it can't be beat!

The Enchantment of Murky Depths

In murky pools where giggles dwell,
Fish wear wigs, and corals yell.
A turtle dressed as a pirate grand,
Swims with a treasure map in hand.

The crabs do dance a funky beat,
While octopuses juggle their own feet.
Bubbles rise like silly balloons,
As minnows sing off-key tunes!

A snail in shades, so cool and sly,
Zooms past a clam who just can't fly.
With bubbles puffed from a blowfish's grin,
The party starts, let the fun begin!

Let laughter echo 'neath the waves,
Where seaweed sways in jellyfish caves.
In this watery world, joy's never late,
We flip and flop, it's quite the fate!

Fragments of Forgotten Waters

In ages past, what did they find?
A fish in glasses, rather unrefined.
A treasure chest filled with rubber ducks,
And all the seaweed dancing like bucks.

An old boot told tales of surf and laugh,
While jellyfish posed for a silly photograph.
The clownfish giggle, donning bow ties,
Sardines wiggle with knowing eyes.

A wise old crab declares a toast,
To the sea cucumbers, who brag the most.
With sea stars playing hopscotch on shells,
And laughter ringing as everyone dwells.

In nostalgic glances, we dive below,
For fragments of fun where the currents flow.
Raise a fin with a splash and shout,
For silly secrets, we can't live without!

Phantoms in the Blue

Ghostly fish with floppy tails,
Swim through bubbles like trailing trails.
With every flip, a giggle spins,
As they dive into sparkling fins.

A sea ghost sings a sea shanty loud,
While clowns make a splash, drawing a crowd.
In a haunted ship, an eel tells jokes,
And the mermaids laugh like silly folks.

The turtles play tag with an old anchor,
While sea horses perform like top dancers.
Waves crash with giggles, a sound so sweet,
As enchanted phantoms twirl on their feet.

So if you peer where the shadows glide,
You might see laughter take you for a ride.
In the blue depths, where the sea plays tricks,
Funny ghosts share their oceanic licks!

Beneath the Tidal Shroud

Under waves, where the stories swim,
A fish wears a hat that's far too dim.
With a grin so wide, they wave around,
A party happening in the ocean's ground.

Starfish play cards, they call it 'shell',
While dolphins laugh at a crab's bad swell.
The barnacles swap their funny tales,
As clams make bets on seaweed trails.

Blowfish puff up, they make the best jest,
While seaweed strings join the underwater fest.
A pirate parrot squawks with delight,
And all of the fish dance into the night.

With bubbles that tickle and foam that sings,
Joyous laughter fills the watery springs.
So come take a dip in those vibrant swells,
Where fun and folly splash like shells!

Whispers of the Deep

In the ocean's wide embrace,
Fish play poker, what a race!
Octopi fold their many hands,
Shark's the dealer, it's in the sands.

The jellyfish glide with grace so fine,
Making puns as they intertwine.
"Stop stinging!" the clownfish cries,
While seahorses wear party ties.

Crabs dance sideways, what a sight,
With a conch shell blaring out at night.
The water's alive with giggles and cheer,
As the starfish join in the smear.

Dolphins dive with a splash and spin,
"Who's the prettiest?" they laugh and grin.
Not a dull moment in this grand spree,
Under waves, it's a party for free!

Secrets of the Liquid Realm

Down in the depths where bubbles roam,
Crustaceans gossip while finding a home.
A walrus jokes with a sly old eel,
"Why are you so slimy? It's quite the deal!"

Mermaids play tricks, steal a few scales,
As darting fish tell curious tales.
"Did you hear the one about the coral tight?
Got snagged in a net during the night!"

The plump pufferfish puffs up with cheer,
"I'm the balloon of the year, I declare!"
Barnacles groan, "We're just stuck here,
While you float away, what a fine career!"

Frogs croak jokes on lily pads high,
While ocean bugs dance, they give it a try.
Surfing on waves they catch the best breeze,
Underwater revelry, a life full of tease!

Echoes from the Aquatic Abyss

In a world where bubbles boldly burst,
The fish tell stories, they're quite the first.
Cementing the tales that float in the blue,
With laughs that echo, it's a jolly crew.

"Why did the turtle cross the reef?"
"Because the fish told him, it's quite a feat!"
Giggling guppies swirl round and round,
As seahorses huddle, their snickers abound.

Anemones sway, tickling the beat,
While crabs compose tunes on waltzing feet.
"There's a disco tonight with glowworms galore,
We'll boogie all night till our shells get sore!"

The dolphins sport shades, so suave and cool,
With schooling fish, they become the school.
Under waves, they dance and sing,
Life in the deep, such a whimsical fling!

Shadows in the Blue Depths

In the twilight zone where giggles are dark,
The squids paint pictures just like Van Gogh's arc.
"Can you see my brush strokes, a masterpiece?"
Said the squishy delight, "Now let's feast!"

Sea cucumbers slide, so low and slow,
While playful otters put on a show.
"Can you juggle?" they ask with a tease,
While fish roll over, they laugh with ease.

A parade of crabs in fancy hats,
Strutting about like fashionable cats.
"Who wore it best?" they quip and sway,
As seaweed cheers, "It's a grand ballet!"

The shadows dance softly, a cheerful throng,
In a whimsical world where all feel they belong.
Under the sea, with laughter that rings,
A comedic ballet of the deep ocean flings!

The Mirage of Coral Dreams

In the reef, the fish all dance,
Wearing outfits, catching glance.
A clownfish jokes, with dots of glee,
He thinks he's funny, but oh dear me!

The coral castles stand so bright,
Pink and purple, quite the sight.
But watch out for the grumpy crab,
He acts tough, but he's just a blab!

An octopus with eight left shoes,
Swims in circles, feeling blues.
He loses track, what a big hoot,
And blames it on his tail-less hoot!

So dive right in, join the fray,
Where laughter bubbles in the sway.
Each splash, a giggle, each seaweed swirl,
In coral dreams, let joy unfurl.

Twists of the Undertow

In the swell, a funny sight,
A dolphin sings with all its might.
With bubble trails and silly flips,
His voice makes waves, all the fish do trips!

The seaweed sways, a dance so grand,
A sea turtle joined, with a clueless hand.
He tried to boogie, but fell with a splash,
And all around him, the fish did dash!

An eel sneezed, oh what a sound,
The bubbles flew and swirled around.
A whale laughed loud, it rumbled deep,
Making waves that rocked us to sleep.

So watch the tide, let giggles sway,
In the current's twist, we laugh away.
For in the dance of water's play,
Funny tales are here to stay.

Veils of the Ocean

Anemones waltz in fancy dress,
With silly smiles, they cause a mess.
A fish with stripes, thinks it's a star,
But swims in circles, not going far!

The jellyfish float in a dreamy trance,
With tentacles waving, they seem to prance.
One gets tangled in a seal's big paw,
They giggle together without a flaw!

A seahorse whisper, 'What's up today?'
Seems there's a party, come join the play!
With bubbles bursting, laughter's the game,
The ocean's veil, it's never the same!

So play along, join the ocean's fun,
Where every creature has jokes by the ton.
With silly antics beneath the tide,
In playful waters, let joy abide.

Whispers of the Siren

A siren sings with a cheeky grin,
Her tune's a mix of mischief and spin.
She lures the sailors with silly rhymes,
But they trip on seaweed, oh dear times!

Her hair flows like currents, tangled and wild,
She twirls and flips, a capricious child.
The fishes snicker, join in the fun,
In this watery realm, laughter's never done!

A hermit crab walks in fancy shoes,
Strutting around with nothing to lose.
But watch him slip on a slick little stone,
Now he's tumbling, completely blown!

So if you hear a siren's song,
Just dance with joy and sing along.
For in these depths, where laughter swells,
The whispers of joy are easy to tell.

Echoing Depths

A fish in a suit, what a sight to see,
He dances like crazy, but can't find his key.
Octopus playing poker, with cards on his tentacle,
Squirting ink at the dealer, it's quite the spectacle.

A clam tells a joke, but it's all in a shell,
The laughter is silent, can't hear it so well.
Dolphins are snickering, flipping with glee,
While turtles play tag, oh what a spree!

A crab does a dance, flips sideways, oh dear,
He trips on a lobster, they both disappear!
And as they emerge, with clumsy delight,
They laugh at the bubbles, what a strange sight!

So if you dive down, take a peek and a glance,
You might just find fish who love to dance!
With jokes in the currents and giggles in streams,
The ocean is filled with hilarious dreams.

The Hushed Tranquility

In silence, the seaweed does jive and sway,
A starfish who's dreaming of a bright cabaret.
Sea turtles with top hats, what a curious crew,
They'make waves in the surf, wishing for déjà vu.

Shrimps with a flash, like tiny disco lights,
Hosting a party, under moonlit nights.
A clam in the corner throws pearls as his game,
While sea anemones beckon, 'Come join our fame!'

A whale sings a tune, but it's off-key, you bet,
The dolphins all giggle, 'A musical threat!'
But deep down they love it, it's joy but absurd,
Singing and dancing, the fish fly in a blur!

So swirl down below, where the laughter does hide,
The ocean's a place where the fun is worldwide!
From bubbles to giggles, it's a comedy show,
Where the playful depths drift in a bubbly glow.

Ghosts of the Deep

A ghostly old mariner floats with his crew,
But they're all laughing, it's quite the hullabaloo!
With fishing rods missing, they're lost in the tide,
Chasing after sea cucumbers, what a wild ride!

An octopus grins, with a hook in his hand,
Declaring, 'I'm lucky, I'm the best in the land!'
His friends roll their eyes, as they drift in the gloom,
Wishing for snacks in the ghostly sea room.

A pirate parrot flaps, looking quite bemused,
Saying, 'What's a sea without treasure to lose?'
But the treasure they find is silly and bright,
Rubber ducks floating, what a ridiculous sight!

So if you see shadows, don't run in a panic,
Just join in their fun, it's quite an oceanic!
With laughter and pranks, they won't cause you fright,
In the ghosts' playful realm, it's sheer delight!

Celestial Reflections

The stars in the water twinkle and gleam,
Fishes are bathers, in bubbles they steam.
A seahorse with shades floats by for a chat,
Sipping on seaweed, how fancy is that?

The jellyfish glide with a glow so bright,
Creating a dance, like a slow, sly night.
While sardines form conga lines with a cheer,
Making waves and laughter, bringing joy near!

A shark tries to tango but trips on a rock,
While turtles just chuckle, ticking like a clock.
'Oh dear!' says the fish, 'We'll have to rehearse,
But let's keep it upbeat, for better or worse!'

So pop on your goggles, and dive with delight,
The cosmic show glimmers, so funny and bright.
In the cosmos below, where joy's intertwined,
The depths of the sea have humor, you'll find!

The Depths of Silence

A fish wore glasses, quite the sight,
Swimming in jeans to feel just right.
He cracked a joke, the seaweed swayed,
In ocean chats, no words delayed.

The turtles laughed, their shells so round,
A starfish danced on sandy ground.
With bubbles popping, a clownfish grinned,
In deep sea antics, the fun won't end.

Submerged Sorrows

A dolphin sighed, life's quite a bore,
Doing handstands while on the floor.
A seahorse giggled, tail tied in knots,
"Why don't we wear these fancy spots?"

A crab with shades gave a low wave,
"Let's start a band, I'll be so brave!"
Yet every tune turned into a splash,
As giggles echoed, in the sea a crash.

Reflections from Below

A jellyfish twirled, a disco ball,
With lights so bright, I had a ball.
Octopuses played cards with flair,
But one lost track, an ink-filled scare.

The fish fished for jokes, what a game,
"I'm hooked on puns," one said with fame.
But every punchline fell with a thud,
At the end, they guffawed, "What a dud!"

The Ocean's Dark Heart

Where shadows play, a creature roams,
Wearing mismatched socks, he's going home.
A whale with flair, a hoot and a sigh,
He sang off-key, oh my, oh my!

A crab in eyeliner, feeling all bold,
With tales so wild, they've never been told.
"Rock the reef!" shouted a clam with pride,
With friends all around, there's nowhere to hide.

The Enigma of Undercurrents

There's a fish wearing glasses, oh what a sight,
It reads the underwater news, day and night.
With bubbles as ink, it scribbles around,
Writing tales of his pals, the strangest you've found.

A crab with a monocle, thinks he's quite sly,
Dancing in circles, but still won't fly.
He claims he's a lawyer, full of great laws,
Yet can't get a grip on his own claws.

The octopus juggles quirky old shells,
While gossiping seaweed, we've all heard its yells.
They tell of a diver who lost his shoe,
Now the fish have a party, is it honoring you?

In deep of the sea, where nobody peeks,
A sandwich floats by, oh the scent it reeks.
They feast on the leftovers, just like it's real,
Undercover snacks, what a fishy meal!

Ghosts Floating in the Blue

In currents where shadows make secrets so sly,
Float whimsical spirits with wings, oh my!
A walrus in white, claims he's quite chic,
But trips on his tusks, oh what a clumsy peak!

The jellyfish giggles, with laughter it glows,
While teasing the seahorse, that thinks he can pose.
They both dance in circles, with grace and delight,
But lose all their rhythm, a bizarre underwater sight.

A clam plays the tambourine, shaking with glee,
While fish don't seem bothered, they're sipping their tea.
The echoes of chuckles bounce off the shore,
As the squad of shellfish applaud and encore.

But the big scary shark lurks, muttering a tune,
Wishing to join in, but just scaring the moon.
So everyone giggles, and hides rather fast,
With humor afloat, who can resist such a blast?

Routes to Hidden Waters

Follow the trails where the bubbles all rise,
Sea turtles get lost in their quest for surprise.
With maps made of seaweed, they fervently search,
For a treasure of laughter, at the edge of the birch.

Starfish flip over, declaring a race,
But turn into cartwheels, oh what a disgrace!
The fish in the reef join the laughter brigade,
While crabs hold a conference, debating their trade.

They stumble on pebbles, all slick and well-glossed,
Swapping tall stories of the treasure they've lost.
The octopus grins, making plans with great zeal,
To start a new journey, for an imaginary meal.

And when the tide whispers, with secrets to share,
The giggles resound, floating back through the air.
In the quest for pure fun, every creature's a part,
In these routes full of whimsy, all join with a heart!

Beneath the Lapping Ripples

Under the waves, where the strange things all blend,
A dolphin dives deep, claiming he's quite the friend.
With a bubble-blowing trick, he makes them all laugh,
While juggling with pearls, he's quite the fine gaff.

The mermaids are knitting with strands of sea grass,
Producing some sweaters that nobody would pass.
But the fish swim on by, striking silly poses,
As the currents tickle, they're a bunch of such roses.

A flounder is fretting, 'I can't find my seat!'
While seahorses tango, they can't skip a beat.
Each ripple that dances, a question of glee,
"Is this sweater on sale? It's too tight for me!"

In the whirl of the catch, they laugh through the flow,
Caught in the chaos, their merriment grows.
And so the adventures, they stumble and twirl,
In the depths of the waves, where humor unfurls!

Choir of the Deep Waters

Bubbles rise and fishies croon,
A gurgling tune by the light of the moon.
Octopus leads with its eight-armed sway,
While crabs clap shells, 'Hip-hip-hooray!'

A dolphin breaks in, adds a flip and a spin,
The starfish all cheer, 'Let the fun times begin!'
Seahorses twirl in a watery dance,
While squids squirt ink, giving laughter a chance.

Corals all giggle in colors so bright,
And turtles with hats join the hilarious sight.
When seaweed starts swaying, they know it's the cue,
For a grand underwater hullabaloo!

As waves softly chuckle, crabs kick up sand,
In this wet little world, it's all perfectly planned.
Their raucous giggles echo through the sea,
In a world where laughter is always carefree.

In the Cradle of the Waves

Sea turtles in boats made of lily leaves,
Sail to the rhythm of fishy reprieves.
Dolphins wear shades, reclining with flair,
While starfish lounge, all without a care.

Jellyfish pop like balloons with a snap,
While mermaids with floats take a whimsical nap.
Bubbles become confetti, swirling about,
As the water throws parties, there's no room for doubt!

Seashells are trumpets, blowing out tunes,
As seasick old whales sing to the moons.
They chuckle and jive, a frolicsome crew,
In this jolly expanse where fun brews anew.

With each gentle wave comes a giggle or two,
As creatures gather round for a straight-up hullabaloo.
In watery halls, where the laughter flows wide,
The humor runs deep, like an oceanic tide.

Shadows Among the Stones

Little fish peek from behind rugged rocks,
Sharing their secrets, swapping their jokes.
A crab with a grin shimmies to the front,
Saying, 'Hey, fishy! Let's go on a hunt!'

They search for lost treasures, a tooth or a shell,
And laugh till they're rolling, oh, wouldn't that sell?
The mermaids join in with a flute made of sea,
Bringing joy, making music more vivid and free!

But watch out for eels, they pop out and tease,
'Where are your problems? Just drop them, please!'
With puns that are slippery, they wiggle and sway,
Adding to the laughter beneath the bay.

Together they delve through the shadows and beams,
In this hidden realm where humor redeems.
With giggles and splashes, they navigate fun,
In the dance of the stones, the laughter's begun!

Caverns of the Sea

In caverns so dark, where the sea urchins joke,
The fickle fish dart, like an underwater cloak.
A treasure chest rumbles, spilling its gold,
While pirate fish laugh, ignoring the cold.

The lobsters declare, 'We're the kings of this cave,'
While jellys inspect all the things that they crave.
Fish with the mustaches go gliding on by,
'Hey, is that a reflection or just a weird spy?'

They dodge and they dart, playing tag like a dream,
In this whimsical world, they're quite the team.
With scoundrels and giggles, the echoes take flight,
In a happy caverns affair, they dance till the night!

So dive in the depths, let giggles unfold,
With treasures abundant, there's joy to behold.
Whatever you find, whatever the charms,
In these silly seas, let laughter cause calm.

www.ingramcontent.com/pod-product-compliance
Lightning Source LLC
Chambersburg PA
CBHW060144230426
43661CB00003B/562